290
$7.99

LIVING AS A LESBIAN

LEARNING RESOURCES CENTER
SANTA FE COMMUNITY COLLEGE

Also by Cheryl Clarke:

Narratives

LIVING AS A LESBIAN

Poetry by Cheryl Clarke

Firebrand
Books
Ithaca, New York

Poems in this book, some in slightly different versions, have appeared previously in *Conditions, Hanging Loose, Ikon, Lady-Unique-Inclination-of-the-Night, The New York City Pride Guide,* and *Sinister Wisdom;* and in the anthology *Lesbian Poetry,* ed. Elly Bulkin and Joan Larkin (Persephone Press, 1981).

Book design by Mary A. Scott
Cover design by Betsy Bayley
Typesetting by Martha J. Waters at the Cornell Daily Sun

Printed in the United States of America by McNaughton & Gunn

Library of Congress Cataloging-in-Publication Data

Clarke, Cheryl, 1947-
    Living as a lesbian.

    1. Lesbianism--Poetry.   2. Afro-American lesbians--Poetry.   I. Title.
PS3553.L314L58 1986   811'.54   86-4648
ISBN 0-932379-13-3 (alk. paper)
ISBN 0-932379-12-5 (pbk. : alk. paper)

dedicated to all the fat or skinny,
black or yella, grinning or toothless
madonnas — live or dead

Contents

10

i.

14th Street was gutted in 1968.
Fire was started on one side of the street.
Flames licked a trail of gasoline to the other side.
For several blocks a gauntlet of flames.
For several days debris smoldered with the stench
of buildings we had known all our lives. Had known
all our lives. I recalled the death of Otis Redding.
My sense of place was cauterized.
Since that time the city has become a buffalo
nearly a dinosaur and,
as with everything else white men have wanted
for themselves,
endangered
or extinct.

wearing my cap backwards

poets are among the first witches
so suffer none to live
or suffer none to be heard
and watch them burn before your eyes
less they recant and speak their verse
in latin.

i'm a poet.
i speaks in pig latin.
i eats pigs feet — a shonuff sign
of satan
to those whose ears are trained to
dactyls and iambs
who resolve all conflicts in couplets.

i run from mice.
mistake dead, brown leaves
scurried by sharp quick breezes
for rats
and write at stop lights
listening to duke ellington
at the cotton club.

an atavistic witch am i.
wearing beads of tarot
searching for wiccas
burning old drafts
chasing dreaded women
covering their locks
til sheba's return.

how like a man

how like a man
is the ku klux klan
it comes in the night
to wag its ugly shaft
to laugh at the final climax of its rape
as rope chokes out the final cry of 'why?'
blood blurring sight of a naked cross.

so like a man
is the ku klux klan to rape and run
wrapped in stained sheets:
an outlaw orgy
a pagan benediction
a twisted crucifixion — not hollywood
nor halloween but some very for-real devils,
underground pigs
crosses between their cloven feet
guarding the spell of flesh burning.

in daylight
how like a man is the ku klux klan:
it sits in the medieval drag of the judge
in the tailored monotony of the jury
and the striped blue gray khaki armor of the
corny knight —
defenders of the cross.

a dying man is the ku klux klan
spurting its last venom on the dungeon floor
like the scum joan little iced:
    'free joan little
    she slayed a grand dragon!'
no more to flex its dick in nature
seeding her with lye.

the knife slices a different way today.
oh, what a man was the k-k-k.

urban gothic

i.
Heads still in a chant from last week's
freedom action,
we bopped down for one o'clock arraignment
to the court
the jailhouse on the highway
bopped on down to that funky rat's nest
on rte. 18 west.

Layin cross the street from the projects —
concrete camp where 246 people of color
spend their confinement contained —
the courthouse belches dark folk
like Squibb labs belches the stench of dog
carcasses.

We are greeted there by a gold-braided knight,
who points us with his night stick to the rear,
quickly shows us the back door
of the jailhouse
the court on the highway.

Immediately we amaze at the congestion and
confusion,
the congestion and confusion of an auction,
perhaps.
A gigolo lounges at the block in a black negligee,
patting gently his black toupee,
adjusting spastically sepia-tinted aviator
spectacles,
nodding to an anglo-french surname
and bidding justice:

'Here a fine, there a fine, everywhere a fine fine.
$25, $50, $100, $500, $1000, $2000, $5000(!)! Come
on up! Pay the clerk! If you got a job you can stay on
the street on the installment plan! If you can't make a
bid you are going, going, gone from the courthouse
to the jail on the highway. Freedom is the chattel
here, at the jail, the courthouse on the highway!'

And poor people
black, purple, umber, burgundy, yellow,
red, olive, and tan people.
In neat-pressed vines.
On crutches.
In drag.
With child and children.
Dissidents, misfits, malcontents, and marginals
serving out our sentences on the streets of
America
spread-eagled against walls and over car hoods.
Frantic
like rats in a maze
an experiment in living
down at the jail,
the courthouse on the highway.

ii.
A young blood,
face, hands, head swaddled like a mummy
in soiled and flesh-tone bandages,
stomach still too sore to pump breath
for speech mouths 'not guilty' to the irony
of assault, faints with ache and nausea
before the giggling demeanor of this feudal
clown.

My comrade grabs my shoulder, presses a nervous
buzzing whisper to my ear and tells me:

> 'They took me, too, last week. By the belt, threw me
> against their car. Punched me, kicked me, cuffed me,
> called me nigger, and made good their promises of
> worse when they got me to the jail, the courthouse
> on the highway. Beat my natural black ass down at
> the jail, the courthouse on the highway.'

iii.
> 'Quiet in the court. I'm the judge. . . .You in the
> black hat . . . I say — you, girl in the black hat . . .
> you — talking in my court. You talking in my court?
> You! talking in my court? Well . . . pay the clerk $25
> for contempt. . . .You don't have it? Why, sergeant,
> take her to the back. And keep her there. What?
> Your children? Well, you should have thought about
> them before you talked in my court. Because I'm the
> judge here, at the jail, the courthouse on the
> highway!'

iv.
From cotton to khaki.
The stultifying odor of concrete replaces the intractable soil of plantations. The gavel refines the whip but not its intent. And that niggers still have no rights white men are bound to respect is still the code of all the costumed fascist hustlers who pimp justice in all the funky courtrooms of America.

And me. And you. Us. With our dumb disbelief. Our liberal grief. Out here in minimum security. Confined to circles of apathy, anger, fear. Living out our lives in the closet of privilege for now.
For now buffered from the routine of 'Let's see some i-dee.' The naked evil will find us too and take us, like a lynch mob, from our closets. In the night or in the day catch us like insanity — unforewarned and unrestrained without summonses, subpoenas, or Miranda rights.
Search us.
Seize us.
And call it routine procedure
down at the jail,
the courthouse on the highway.

auction

January 8, 1979: Charles Mingus is dead and I've just spent a day at the auction bidding on turn of the century artifacts because jazz is too awesome for me these days.

But I will rub the aboriginal turquoise against me for strength to listen to you strain the blues through your bear paws.

Let the primal clarity ring me, ring me deep.

acceptance

You say to me, 'I need you to let me die,'
and months of denial are transformed into
acceptance. I begin to see your funeral
barge carried off the Cape into the primordial
Atlantic.

Ears and wrists dressed in the aboriginal
turquoise and coral for healing and protection.
For warmth, winter jacket with quetzal images.
The journey may take many months.

Red dice tucked into your fist for diversion
and to keep your wits sharp.
Ashanti pendant in your other hand
for perpetuity and regeneration.

And then you say to me, 'I want to be cremated.'

living as a lesbian on the make

Straight bars ain't so bad
though filled with men
cigarette smoke
and juke noises.
A martini straight up and jazz
can take me beyond their static.
Alone she came in denim and a
magenta tee
hair cut to a duck tail
ordered Miller's and smoked two
kinds of cigarettes
sat at a table close but distant
was pretty and I was lonely
and knew she was looking for a woman.
All through the set I looked at her
until she split in the middle of it.
I almost followed her out but was too
horny to leave the easy man talking
loud shit to me for a seduction I'd
have to work at.
The music sounding tasty
saxophone flugelhorn bass and drums
hitting familiar riffs
the titles escaping me.

the layoff

A blizzard struck New Jersey like a tornado.
Snow accumulated like Chicago.
I saw a streak of lightning.
Someone else heard thunder.
I am earth and burned everything
I cooked tonight.
Managed to salvage a good slave's supper:
hoecake, turnip greens, navy beans.
In a month I get laid off.

Marijuana isn't what it used to be.
So I learn from poetry to reach for
the brief epiphany.

My parents each made their own money.
Raised me to make mine.
Worked at one job
in one office
in one building
slept in one bed for 35 years
so I could have choices.

Marijuana isn't what it used to be.

My sister the goddess of speech
got laid off last month.
She has a child.
And I want what's good for my poetry.

By turns I feel proud
politically correct
of the masses
then humiliated
humbled
and by turns
find myself in a daze
rapt
on how I'll put gas in my car past June.
I want to hear no anecdotes about those
who have less.

Marijuana isn't what it used to be in this
era of the nuclear renaissance white boy.

A storm hit us like an earthquake.
There was lightning.
Then thunder.
The week before in a lesser storm
many deaths on the Turnpike.
Road workers had been laid off that week.
I tell myself to think of those who must
live on less.

Marijuana isn't what it used to be.

A friend tells me the soil is impotent
the plants sprayed with pesticides
expect a light head
cling to the ritual of passing it between us.

ii.

The woman who raised me asks me
'Where is the hope here, where is the hope?
The fruit here is rotten.
All the roots are excavated.
The sidewalks are cracked and in pieces
and the rain forms stagnant pools.
Children walk the night through the streets here
and men make every urge so public.
And who will hear me cry for help?
Will they want to climb all these flights
up here to save me? And what will you do
when you wake up
and find your good woman
gone?'*

*Line adapted from blues songs sung by Bessie Smith, 1925-1927, *Bessie Smith: Nobody's Blues But Mine* (Columbia Records, reissued 1972).

journal entry: sisters

The two of them are obviously close and not often together. They give the impression of stolen moments, hidden lives. There is a story to these rendezvous. The low tones. The tentative eyes.

The seductive friendliness of the younger-looking one — dyed dark, too dark, cascading curls, pretty face — offering to light the cigarette of a stranger at a nearby table.

The quick peripheral glances of the plain, prematurely white-haired one — tomboyish, near sixty.

Who knows what they say to one another. They talk very little. It's their way, to be with one another in whatever way they want to be. And all that's good to be is not necessarily good to talk.

The plain one looks at her neatly clipped nails. The pretty one surveys surroundings and says: 'I have my grandchildren this weekend.' The plain one nods and looks downward, over her shoulder, out the window. 'There's your sister. Better go now,' says the pretty one making herself small in the booth, offering the book of matches to the stranger.

Her friend slides past her out the booth, hurries slump shouldered to meet a yet older, more white-haired woman, beckoning for her arm.

for my mother, 1979

Life in the rugged west does not
reconcile loss — quick, immediate, visceral.
Futurism, infinity, heart transplants — any mass
produced gadget of immortality —
thwart the reckoning.

My mother lost her right breast and best friend
in two months of one another this winter.
She prepares to lose the first, to sacrifice
the part for the whole.
The second is not even foreshadowed but in
the symbol of the foregone fall.
Severances.
Flash floods.
Earthquakes.
A tree split from her branches by lightning.
Unceremoniously abrupt.
To wake on an afternoon to an anesthetized cavity.
Two months later at dawn to news of flames tagging a robe.
The pain of the latter not so splendidly dulled.
And summer is lonely with prosthesis and surrogate intimacy.

palm leaf of Mary Magdalene

Obsessed by betrayal
compelled by passion
I pull this mutant palm leaf, orange
from my childhood of palm sundays.
Weave it into a cross, pray to it,
wear it as headband and wristband,
strap it round my ankle.
Magical as the pentecostal holy ghost.
Turning to fuchsia in afternoon light.

More than once an olive skinned nun pulled her
skirts up for me; later bribed me with a wild
orange palm leaf; thought its color a miracle
awesome as the resurrection; whispered it was
the palm leaf of Mary Magdalene, laughed;
side to side, stroked her unfrocked breasts
and shoulders with it; tied my wrist to hers
with it and took my forgiveness.

Mary Magdalene's palm leaf to you, dearest whore.
Flash it cross your sex back and forth like a
shoe shine rag more gently with as much dedication
while I (and the one you sleep with tonight instead
of me) watch and wait for the miracle
weave it into a cross pray to it
wear it as headband and wristband
tie your ankle to the bedpost with it
tongue of the holy ghost
palm leaf of Mary Magdalene.

freedom flesh
(for Assata)

had you not chosen the dangerous business of
freedom you could be walking barefoot in the
red hills of North Carolina hand in hand with
Kakuya instead of assuming disguises and aliases
traveling through subway stations camping in
sacred aboriginal territory.
you could have been a school marm
graduate student
community organizer
instead of an underground railroad
conductor
picture seen in post offices
or on hastily drafted posters advertising
liberation.

you could have continued giving yourself
guitar lessons
writing political poems
or become a public speaker
instead of ex-political prisoner
paradox   irony   phenomenon
flesh of freedom.

Revised July, 1985

29

funeral thoughts

You treat people like you're taught in your family.
And let them treat you the way your family did.
No matter what other ways you learn
what your family teaches hangs tough.
There are always those you
adore   take for granted   fear   control
coerce   seduce   confess to and tell everything
and those who die before you get the chance.

I know now I could have told him anything.
Instead in panic of ecstasy
I learned not to fear the body I came from.
I touch myself and faded color prints
project themselves:
        the spinet
        the victrola
        the console
        fitted taffeta
        strapless
        cut to the cleavage
        black silk and stiff cotton
        and muslin
        a red rose in one hand
        and the other
        softly and mysteriously
        between her naked arm
        and constricted waist.
        My own hand steadying the camera.

I know now I could have told him anything
with his fragility and crying
so like the purple irises he planted
each year had she not been so awesome
and demanding bribing me out of his
confidence
with handmade dolls
and handsewn dresses
buying his underwear
choosing his friends
and making decisions.

In his garden
in his car
on the ball field
I could have told him anything.
Instead I hoarded their cast-off clothes
boldly removing them from her shopping bags
for the needy
storing them back with me
to marvel at their intricacy
in the chamber of fantasy
that kept my desire.

Even though he was quiet
with the dough
he was always kneading
mornings before he slept
I could have told him anything.
Even that I never lost my lust
for her years after refusing to be
fitted for the patterns she was
always cutting.

Nights I watched him leave for the
night shift and her leave later
with the voices of women.
Nights·
after I grew tall as her
she called to me not to sleep alone
on the sheets she embroidered
in the basement room he built for me
where lovers defied their parents
and stole to me.
Nights she turned to me
careful of boundaries
fretful
wanting.

Nights turning to her
strong and in anger
to lift the shift
over her body
to press myself between her.
Even of that I could have told him
but he was satisfied with things
and slept during the day.

Revised July, 1985

palm reading

To soften the terror of living
the old black witch does not tell
me everything at once.
She withholds the unwholesome forecast.
It catches in her throat
and dissolves into a telling of the
ravaged past:
      'dissected trees, dismantled houses, violated genitals . . .
      crowded crossings, unwelcomed landings . . .
      forced, futile toil . . .
      the pillage of the soul . . .
      in spite of the mutilations, the vibrations
                is very strong . . .
      and there is yet some grace for the future.'

The old black witch keeps her sources well
and does not tell me everything at once.
Holds back the unwholesome forecast.
Retells the ravaged past.
Closes her misty eyes to the lines,
tightens her fist against her teeth,
draws in her breath,
gives me back my hand,
and does not tell me everything
at once.

Revised March, 1982

storyteller
(for Grace Paley)

I like you both.
I want to take you together
to a diner.
After, I know a place where Anna Magnani plays
every night.
No subtitles.
Then a place beatniks swing til dawn.
I'll sit between you both
my arms around you
at the same time
you'll rest your heads on me.

At dawn we'll make a closed circle
and say every word
stolen from us
and still forbidden
very loud.

All you need is a clap to get into this song.*

Wild children
hungry women
with no rhymes
I'll rob your dreams with purple poems.
I'll cook cornbread in an iron skillet,
and matzo brie.

*From a live recording by Stevie Wonder.

Indira

Posed on the bed of the aging, antlike
Gandhi, a Hindu not a Brahmin
not father nor namesake.
A name you chose, neither Brahmin
nor Hindu.
An aura that confused who you were.
You could have been my own mother
trapped in the violence of some man
she sees every day.
Hostess and harridan.

By sheer dint of rhetoric
saved a Muslim from a lynch mob
in '47, the year I was born.
All noblesse oblige with peasants
pleading their misery to you
in your courtyard daily.
Bright silks drawn tight for protocol.
Princess and dynast.

A rock out of a mob in Orissa!
Nose broken, lip gashed.
Draw your veil over the mess of
blood and pulp.
Refuse to leave the podium.
Victory in Delhi!
A garland of marigolds placed
round your neck by an enemy.
Sit smiling despite your allergy.
Populist and aristocrat.

Two hundred prison letters from
Jawaharlal the Jewel, the democrat,
the atheist you defied in death
with a Hindu funeral
and banned his writings during the
'Emergency.'
Your mother warned you about men,
and you were much in their company.
It's cruel you had only sons, loved
the ruthless one, didn't trust the
other. Who else besides your Sikh
bodyguard knew you wouldn't wear your
vest under orange sari bloodsoaked?
Autocrat and neofascist.

Surrounded by men all your life and
parliaments and cabinets and sycophants.
Nurtured, counseled, schooled, scolded,
ridiculed, and jailed by men, and praying
for the blessings men in power pray for:
    multinationals
    wars
    nukes
    spaceships
    immortality.
Still you could have been a woman in
my own family caught in the violence
of some man in her neighborhood.
Pragmatist and despot.

Funeral bier a flotation tank of
marigolds.
You in purple sari gold-embellished.
The press could've asked me instead
of Margaret Thatcher how I felt about
your murder — brutal, grisly, male.
After all I've known you all my life.
Black eyes studding the front pages
since before I cared a dark woman
could come to power.
But still, what goes around
comes around.
Joan of Arc and Catherine the Great.

Sikhs in New York cheer your demise,
in India they are massacred by the
thousands.
Rajiv finds a charred gold ring in
your ashes, washes his hands of
Bhopal, lunches with multinationals.
Wife burnings occur weekly in India —
a practice, it was reported, that
disgusted you.

journal entry: the weekend my lover is away

Looked forward to it for weeks.
Alone for a whole weekend.
For a whole weekend by myself.
Tried to convince me to be with her.
Am stalwart.

I am in New Jersey.
You are in Ohio.
I am stoned.
You are pitching a tent.
I am writing in my journal
piling books by my side of the bed
television as background
visions of New York City in the morning.
You are poking a campfire.

Anxious that I'm here without her.

I have checked the screens
am scared about the two in the basement
that cannot latch.
Scared of noises I'm scared of every night
but can't turn to you and say, 'It's the
cat jumping against the screen.'

Not feeling reassured.

Police are hysterical lately
over a shooting in Queens.
State police packing the Turnpike
salivating over an alleged 15 car
caravan of the BLA sworn to kill
Jersey cops.
I bailed Butch out of jail for shoplifting
my nephew snores too soundly in the next room
your daughter kicks the wall in her sleep.

Wearing my clothes to bed.
Double checking the doors.
Starting at headlights
that don't pass.

no more encomiums

This anger so visceral I could shit it
and still be constipated.
My ass is sore with the politics
of understanding the best given the circumstances.
I could spit this anger
and still choke on the phlegm
of memories.
Afraid, jealous, or stuck in some foaming
funk I learned from her in the circumstances
of her loneliness, I push away from my lover.
This hotness, this coldness still
in her aging she tricks me.

Sweet words and warm this time —
not like the last time salty and frigid
over some money I owed her —
telling me she's missing me, of the old days,
the pta meetings, Atlantic City in summers.
My stomach turns every day at 4:30
remembering anticipation of the hammer sound
of her spikes on the front porch
when in spite of herself
she was my champion
my song, my soul, my beauty.

Given the circumstances of her crowded life
I can't publish this poem.
She sits on her bed working her
crossword puzzle searching back over 64
years of words to fit the boxes.
And me sulking over 33 years of anger
edited for the space of these lines.
Hounding anger like cunt hurts to fuck,
carnal anger and dreams over too soon.

In the dry heave of Arizona, in a tent,
in the middle of the scarlet streaked day,
I had this dream of her: she cursed me and
I determined I'd tell her she hurt me. I
rehearsed it. Yes, in the very dream I
rehearsed the words I'd say to her —
in spite of the circumstances and fuck
the circumstances —
to finally stand up for myself, to say:
'You hurt me and you always hurt me.'

I can only write this poem, my bilious anger.
This third person, my anger.
Visceral.
I could shit it
spit it
fuck it.
Phlegmatic and choleric,
she hurts my fucking
cunt.
My champion
my song
my soul
my beauty.

iii.

I come to the city for protection
and to witness the thick transactions
of women
and women
and dance with my head.
My turns are calculated
to end on the right foot
to subdue the hip movements.
The city fumes with expectations
and the smells of women
wanting women.
I been in love
six times in the last six months
and ain't done tryin yet.*

*Lines adapted from blues songs sung by Bessie Smith, 1925-1927, *Bessie Smith: Nobody's Blues But Mine* (Columbia Records, reissued 1972).

journal entry: the last postcard

away from the crush of europeans outside the city
behind a nuke power plant I find my lover who
follows a woman beckoning to her from behind
a coconut tree leading her the hem of her dress
damp her ankles sand sparkling
we pass cows I pause to photograph their ruddy
bovinity to commune with them to lay with them to
straddle one of them
but must run to catch my lover and the relentless
woman who leads her like a drum major calves
flexing like a drum roll I see the first stars
and begin to worry about the way back the stars
are legion and so are the mosquitoes her cabin is
narrow there are sleeping children from the porch
I see her offer my lover a palm wine they make a
fire on the beach fondle yams squash bananas talk
of size consistency taste cook fish feed themselves
and each other with hands and mouths and are not
restrained I watch
the relentless woman asks for my hand
and examines the matrix of my turquoise and
the etchings in its setting knows the meaning of
sunrays is constancy insists on kinships at dawn
she swims dresses and must go early to
market my lover and I feed her before she
leaves and cut coconuts for her daughters
when they wake.

great expectations

questing a lesbian adventure one splendid night
of furtive, fixed stars and fully intend-
ing to have you suck my breasts and fuck me
til dawn called raunchy elizabeth to the window
of your brooklyn apartment saxophone and dolphin-
song muting the rudeness of engines

dreaming the encounter intense as engines
first me then you oh what a night
of rapture and risk and dolphin
acrobatics after years of intend-
ing to find my lesbian sources in the window
of longing wide open in me

fearing failing and wanting to do it again faked me
out — anxious wanting revved like 500 engines
inside your brooklyn apartment window
my body a pillar yours a furnace that curious night
of lesbian lore and fully intend-
ing to play an easy rider to your dolphin-

song. instead of asking you to dive on me dolphin-
like, butch stories hushed the lesbian lust in me
across that expanse of sofa and fully intend-
ing to make you make me like diesel engines
and taking you back over and over into the night
across your expanse of ass in front of the window.

trading passionate conquest tales and at your window
cobalt night grew pink in the stink, the dolphin
wearying wary of heroics asking for clarity all night
instead of covering face with cunt and entering me
low then spectacularly like rocket engines
you panicked the funky passion i fully intend-

ed. yeah, yeah, a funky passion i fully intend-
ed all over the floors walls to the cobalt window
of your brooklyn bedroom til the whine of cold engines
muted the saxophone and called the dolphin
back to sea and your lesbian wetness drying sticky on me
night of furtive, fixed stars oh venus in taurus night.

fully intending to have my way but having no dolphin-
like clarity and the window sticking in me —
a sounding fire engine gridlocked on a windy night.

Vicki and Daphne

Being given a lover's key is an intimate gesture: without it one can figure what course the relationship will take; with it, trust is a temptation.

Blood of the cut from a serrated knife blotted by a slice of cake frosted white and garnished with a sugar molded rose the same color red as her blood set Vicki to musing on the risk she'd taken coming from an office party without warning with half a cake to persuade Daphne.

No bandages in Daphne's medicine cabinet or night table. (Daphne never had what Vicki needed when she needed it. But Vicki was an ex-Marine and compensated by being relentlessly adaptable.) So, she scissored a sanitary pad down to the size of a Curad (to her amazement Daph did have pads) and taped it round her hemorrhaging finger with Daph's last bit of scotch tape.

Vicki's feet hurt in her business pumps. Her business suit pinched her waist and pressed her breasts. The scent of perfume and deodorant mixed with the odor emanating from her pits. She didn't want to get too comfortable. She preferred to await Daphne's pleasure. Her feet might swell or Daph might want her to book.

Vicki removes one shoe and slides the other off her burning heel. (She carries sneakers in her bag but can't really stand the way treads look with nylons.) All day she'd been driven by lust for Daphne. She'd left messages by everyone who might see or speak to Daph to tell her she wanted her.

Where is Daphne? Surely she'd be home soon so Vicki could take off her clothes and complain about her aching pussy.

Being in Daphne's apartment at 11 p.m. without warning and Daphne not home but imminent, fantasy o'ertakes Vicki.
The sound of Daph's
keys in both holes
turning noisily
the house dark
Daphne comes for Vicki where she sits
runs her hand along her nylons
and beyond
Vicki guides her hand

Her throbbing finger draws her back to the reality of her situation: fully clothed, horny, and without warning, and how would she be able to take Daph up the cunt with her middle finger bandaged bulkily? She couldn't even stand air on the wound. Could she Daphne's salty cunt? And her right hand was not so dextrous.

Does Daphne come? Vicki prepares an appropriately humble expression and the honest explanation: *Baby, I'm gonna keep on lovin you til the day I die, cuz I love the way you satisfy.* *

No keys in holes.
No Daphne.
Only next door neighbor fumbling.

*Sung by B.B. King.

48

Without warning, Vicki feels cramps. Her ankles swell. Her finger bleeds every time she flexes. Her pussy is gamey with secretions. She wants to lie down. But Daph hates wrinkled bed clothes.

Vicki falls into a daze, limps to Daph's bed and pulls backs its comforter and top sheet limps then to an odd chest of drawers and removes a small object of comfort. After pulling her skirt to her crotch, lies face down on Daph's bed and applies it to her genital eleven times calling Daph a whore sweetly and being Daph calling herself a bitch roughly.

Vicki sleeps deeply in suit, nylons, and one pump, awaking at 6 a.m. without warning, without Daphne returns the object to its place pulls top sheet and comforter over passion and menses stained sheets smooths her wrinkles brushes the lint.

fall journal entry: 1983

Sharon
25
white
wearing pastel bathrobe
pastel nighties
matching terry slippers

                                            falling
from her Riverside window
left thigh
on recently pruned thicket stump
impaled.

No blood from head or mouth
or certain hole.

Rescuers plentiful
and sincere
in earnest
running to each other
with news
and speculation
of ambulances,
an open 4th floor window,
the thing through her thigh.

A woman stroking Sharon
talking soft to her
telling Sharon her name
the names of her children
where she lives
and 'yes, it's gotten chilly . . .'

the doorman old and afraid
bringing blankets.

Sirens all the way
                              down
to the river
fierce and angry
police burning rubber:
        'Who saw what happened here?
                    'Who saw what happened
here?!
                        'Who saw what happened
here, people?   How can anybody
                              fall
out of a window?'

Blood droplets stain the stump
where medics cut it clean
removing Sharon
gauze wrappings
littering the place where she was.

Who loved Sharon that morning?
Was angry at her?
Hadn't seen her in a long time?
Owed her money?
Who'd she owe money?
Who was she about to make friends with?
Who was on her way over to spend the night?
Was somebody in the room when she
                              fell
jumped
                   or was pushed
from her 4th floor window,
6th floor window?
impaled
burst inside
died
holding it all together
on the outside.

iv.

Intimacy no luxury here.
Telephones cannot be left off the hook
or lines too long engaged
or conversations censored any longer.
No time to stare at our hands
afraid to extend them
or once held
afraid to let go.
We are here.
After years of separation
women take their time
dispose of old animosities.
Tribadism is an ancient panacea and cost efficient
an ancient panacea and cost efficient.

living as a lesbian in the journal
(for J.L.G.)

3/18
. . . and I hate for the party to be over: the anticipation, the long drives, the coffee, the women who like me, the hard, fast sleep, the food. Truth is I don't want to be by myself.

3/19
She wants an adventure.
Go to Africa again.
August maybe.
This time to Kenya and Tanzania.
Take a side trip to Mombasa
where nights the screams of captives
can still be heard.
Mombasa — must go there
and worship what we cannot see.
With naked eye search the sky
for the dark star.

3/20
Words, reefer, and blood passed between us. It was way early in the day and sunny and almost spring. Right then I begin to dread the long drive back and smoke the roach that bears your lipstick's trace.
We have an understanding,
the timing of comediennes,
and the lyrics of 45s
stacked in basements and tenements.
We learned wit from t.v. when it first
took the place of vaudeville.

. . . rock 'n' roll gives me the voice I wished for when I believed in radio. The words come back. The words come back. I sing to myself all the way to Philadelphia. Say poems. Pray to Moms Mabley, Big Maybelle, and other lesser known fat or skinny, black or yella, grinning or toothless madonnas — live or dead.

3/21
There was a time when I would have given my blood to Aretha Franklin. But not now. Not now. Not since she went to South Africa. After Detroit, Chicago, Philadelphia. After the Regal, the Howard, the Apollo. How could she sing in South Africa? All those victim songs come home to roost. And I long for the blood she had in 1967 and will always hold that time sacred marking the emptiness of the singing since the death of Otis Redding.

3/21 (late)
The singer had not lifted her voice in years.
Women said she'd stopped singing.
She sang this night and couldn't stop
like that woman who met you on the street
way early in the day and couldn't stop
talking, asked you how you did your dread
passed on
leaving you with her beauty for the rest of
the day.
The singer sang til her throat was dry
as dust and couldn't stop
and we didn't want her to.

nothing

Nothing I wouldn't do for the woman I sleep with
when nobody satisfy me the way she do.

kiss her in public places
win the lottery
take her in the ass
in a train lavatory
sleep three in a single bed
have a baby
to keep her wanting me.

wear leather underwear
remember my dreams
make plans and schemes
go down on her in front of her
other lover
give my jewelry away
to keep her wanting me.

sell my car
tie her to the bed post and
spank her
lie to my mother
let her watch me fuck my other lover
miss my only sister's wedding
to keep her wanting me.

buy her cocaine
show her the pleasure in danger
bargain
let her dress me in colorful costumes
of low cleavage and slit to the crotch
giving easy access
to keep her wanting me.

Nothing I wouldn't do for the woman I sleep with
when nobody satisfy me the way she do.

what goes around comes around
or the proof is in the pudding

*Truthfulness, honor, is not something which springs ablaze
of itself; it has to be created between people . . . .*
Adrienne Rich, "Women and Honor"

A woman in my shower crying.
All I can do is make potato salad
and wish I hadn't been caught lying.

I dust the chicken for frying
pretending my real feelings too much a challenge
to the woman in my shower crying.

I forget to boil the eggs, time is flying,
my feet are tired, my nerves frazzled,
and I wish I hadn't been caught lying.

Secondary relationships are trying.
I'd rather roll dough than be hassled
by women in my shower crying.

Truth is clarifying.
Pity it's not more like butter.
I wish I hadn't been caught lying.

Ain't no point denying,
my soufflé won't even flutter.
I withhold from the woman in my shower crying
afraid of the void I filled with lying.

V.

We are everywhere and white people still do not see us.
They force us from sidewalks.
Mistake us for men.
Expect us to give up our seats to them on the bus.
Challenge us with their faces.
Are afraid of us in groups.
Thus the brutal one on one.
Like a t.v. news script, every transaction frustrates
rage. Hand in hand with me
you admonish
not to let them come between us
not to let them come between us on the street.
We are struck by war crazy men
recording their gunfire on stereo cassette decks.

journal entry: qualification
(I'm a compulsive overeater and this poem is about that.)

it began for me like many others:
not having for long periods
not having at critical moments
having too much in too short a space.
i wanted comfort
stroking
someone to sleep with
when my sister ran away.

having had i knew the ways of comfort
touching.
i taught myself to get it how i could
on the run
quick
as much as i could stuff into me
at once.

eating became
the central
the rising
the falling
action of my life.
comfort, joy, success
whet my appetite for more.
and marijuana.
i wanted everything at once
giving to get more.

mornings:
the pot first —
the best friend since my sister
always calling me
making me feel good
making me miss her,
taking risks to have her.
music next — essential to poetry.
then a fried yolky gravy
burst all over
that bland dixie delicacy
half a pound of breakfast meat
on the side
any mix of sugar, white flour, butter
baked and dunked in four cups of coffee
before noon.

noon:
extra mayo
extra cheese
on any form of white dough
and coke and pepsi.
chocolate, vanilla, strawberry dairy sweet
a good taurus comfort on low days.

midafternoon raids on the vending machines:
more pernicious than one-armed bandits.
driven by desire for what i would
consume later.
feeling good.
appetites primed.

people are food.
food is people.
one or the other. or both.
both.
i didn't know it for a long time:
when who i want denies me
i eat something
buy something
smoke something.

if i don't have a lover, i eat,
listen to blues, won't write
and am never home.
if i have a lover,
i eat, play rock 'n' roll, write love poems
and take many sick days.

one night after a day of not getting what
and who i wanted — (much like today) —
during a nicotine jag
a caffeine binge
a streak of intense doping
the music loud and constant
with otis redding who reminds me
of potato chips and beer nuts
i turned to the refrigerator:
nothing.
and no gas to drive to the 24 hour
gourmet foodtown but half a jar
of peanut butter
and 23 stale breadsticks.
i ran out of peanut butter
before i ran out of breadsticks
vowing each to be the last
dancing between record player
and breadbox
night fast approaching dawn
for every toke i took
every sip of coffee
every record i spun
i ate.

after three hours of sleep
i amazed at my amusing loss of control.
got up.
began the daily regime without breakfast.
made up for it at lunch in honor of
someone's leaving.
went to the working class foodtown.
avoided the peanut butter shelf.
bought matzos.
picked up a pack of marlboros, hardpack regular.
copped some reefer.
and came to you with
my compulsions full-blown.

it began for me like many others
calling you late at night
for language and intellect
two irresistible foods
after so much dulling.

the urge to consume never leaves.
i'm learning to take my time
instead of swallowing you whole,
to resist projecting to the end of
fucking
so i can raid the cupboard
smoke a cigarette
and pass off into dreams
of sugar, dough, caffeine
light and sweet.

Revised July, 1985

the change

She used to smile, small talk, almost flirt
speaks only if I speak first, swells like cow
udder wanting a milking, acts real curt.
Her countenance is hard toward me now.
Speaks tersely to me, to you kowtows
when she meets us in the hallway.
Impertinent, rude, and untoward now,
your neighbor used to be more friendly.

Your cat died. She found you a kitten
before you'd grieved properly. That, I thought
nervy, but I'm prone to suspicion.
Her countenance is hard toward me now,
throwing smiles like flowers at you and frowns
like needles at me.
The mangy kitten's a cat now. I vow —
your neighbor used to be more friendly.

Who is this woman? Who is she to you?
Bringing tonics to quicken your prow-
ess. Try my chili seasoned high, hot, and true.
Her countenance is hard toward me now.
You smile, turn from me, lead me to the couch.
Not to worry, not to worry.
I go down on you and chew
your clit. She used to be more friendly.

Me on top of you on top of the couch.
Her countenance is hard toward me now.
You give her good cause to cut her eyes at me.
Your neighbor used to be more friendly.

San Juan: 1979

first night:
I am reaffirmed in the dissipating lushness
of this steamy city
where dark men people its sidewalks
and coffee houses,
where pasty gringos meander in twos like nuns
arrogant in their ignorance of the language.

restaurant:
A mulatto waiter seats me resentfully.
Two dark women with Asian eyes seat themselves.
I watch the one. Her eyes go soft and dark at the
other over the candle.

hotel lobby:
I am smug in this scene of seasonal affection
and evening gear, as two dark women with Asian eyes
skate across the marble lobby.
The other is laughing with the one whose eyes went
soft and dark over the candle.

departure:
I am on the tourist shuttle.
Through my Pentax, my eye catches them
in a gray blue blur of three-piece suits
and luggage.
My finger is sluggish.
The unruly head of a tourist
blocks the potential print.
The jitney jerks into gear.

resolution:
I am reaffirmed and ramified
in this noisy, polluted, disappointing city.
Sidewalks crowded with delicate dark men
and sun sick gringos who think the language
quaint and unimportant.

sexual preference

I'm a queer lesbian.
Please don't go down on me yet.
I do not prefer cunnilingus.
(There's room for me in the movement.)

Your tongue does not have to prove its prowess
there
to me
now
or even on the first night.

Your mouth all over my body
then there.

vi.

Since my lover left the city without warning
for a less carcinogenic zone
some place in the desert
where she can stop hating her own people,
my sister passes the night with me
who'd rather be drowning in the deep
blue sea. My lover having left the city without
warning, my sister passes the night with me
and speaks of the murders of Hampton and Silkwood
of the blood of Santiago and Soweto.
Stores her handgun in the night table
passes the night with me and plays the record
player loud. And I remember the words
of a lost slave song.

Miami: 1980

Andy Young and Jesse Jackson are summoned to be firemen. In an election year Carter sends his attorney general. The Florida governor pleads only for a night of brotherhood and sends in 3500 national guardsmen.

In Vancouver, Washington, not even a forest ranger can be found.

(and what to make of Vernon Jordan shot in Fort Wayne, Indiana, and a mysterious blond who cannot be teased out of seclusion.)

Since Menendez tricked African artisans and agriculturists to settle St. Augustine in 1565, later to be counted among Florida's 40,000-odd slaves — where Maroons and Seminoles protected their vengeance in swamps, where a displaced bourgeoisie can find asylum 100 years later, a freak place where a ship can destroy a bridge toppling a busload of people to death by water, where an abomination like Anita Bryant can fester and become a Disney World hero — Florida has been a real fantasia.

Jacksonville is the scene of a memorably ruthless episode over lunch counters in 1960 and '64.

Daytona Beach 1926: blacks are made to carry passes after dark.

(however in that same year a hurricane strikes Miami and blacks are forced by armed marines into the work of reclamation. A black woman is shot by one of them for protesting.)

Miami 1939: men in ritual costume burn 25 crosses and parade through the black section carrying effigies and signs saying: 'the klan will ride again in Florida if niggers try to vote.'

In Tampa 1980 an all-white jury acquits 4 Miami pigs for beating Arthur MacDuffie to death for forgetting that niggers have no rights white men are bound to respect.

Today 16 are dead in Miami
and skies are not yet darkened by Mount St. Helens
ending 100 years of silence with molten rock
burning to ash over Western skies
balancing the account.

Miami will stink with unfound corpses
and so will Vancouver, Washington
so totally surprised a volcano
can find her voice in the new world.

White sidewalks and buildings sprayed with blood
white people claiming innocence of their fathers' transgressions
white women in pin curlers bearing babies and rifles on their
     backs
Arthur MacDuffie's mother begging Liberty City blacks to be
     more longsuffering:
          'Turn to God. Turn to God.'

Liberty City.
Liberty City?

News reports label Miami's violence 'grisly.'
But vengeance is grisly.
The U.S. will die by fire yet.

Observers repeat the fallacy about history.

Others feel we need a good ole fashion
riot to shake our complacency.

I hope not another Detroit.
They never finished finding bodies in Newark.

And no matter how hard they try to make her
a tourist attraction
Mount St. Helens may yet grumble another
hundred years.

Revised December, 1984

living as a lesbian underground:
a futuristic fantasy

in basements
attics
alleyways
and tents
fugitive slaves
poets and griots
seminoles from Songhay
vodun queens —
all in drag,
stumbling over discarded fetuses
hitching
dodging state troopers behind shades
searching for safe houses
uptight but cool:
>   the tam
>   the aviator frame
>   the propped cigarette
>   and singing:
>   'I was born in Georgia.
>   My ways are underground.
>   If you mistreat me,
>   I'll hunt you like a hound.'*

Lack of money produces such atavism.

*"The Honey Man Blues," as sung by Bessie Smith.

But . . . don't be taken in your sleep now.
Call your assassin's name now.
Leave signs of struggle.
Leave signs of triumph.
And run
cept don't stop in Chicago
to give yourself up to a pimp.
Leave signs.

And . . . don't be taken on the nod now.
The Arabs are only a temporary phobia.
It's a short trip from Nyack to the
shores of Tripoli and back.
Thewitchhuntisbuildinghere.
Where you gon be standin when it come?
Leave signs.

And . . . don't get caught sleeping with
your shoes off
while women are forced back to the shelter
of homicidal husbands
rapists are forced to pay child support
children of lesbians orphaned
and blacks, browns, and tans
herded into wire fences somewhere
round Tucson.
Listen for footsteps.
Leave signs.

Travel light
and don't wait til morning.
Qadaffi is only a fleeting distraction
radiating the 3rd world with his
macho, mercurial, maligned smile.
A scapegoat.
Uptight but cool.
The terror is here somewhere
in Detroit.

And . . . don't sleep before midnight.
And don't fret over the Poles.
We in the same fix
with the Pope's position on lust
and family protection
a storefront on every corner
in Manhattan.

Don't be no fool, now, cool.
Imperialism by any other name
is imperialism.
Even Vietnam was finally over.
It's all the same —
a-rabs, gooks, wogs, queers —
a nigger by any other name . . .
Johannesburg is Jamesburg, New Jersey.
Apartheid is the board of education
in Canarsie.

So . . . don't be taken in your sleep now.
Call your assailant's name now.
Leave the building empty
the doors unlocked
and raise the windows high
when they pass by.
Leave signs of struggle.
Leave signs of triumph.
And leave signs.

sister of famous artist brother

a bizarre poetry — tabloids
cash register receipts
but less honest
never the sum
always the parts.
hadn't been for 'famous artist brother's'
name dominating the coverage
might not have known you were
stabbed to death in 'posh pad.'
and whose business was it anyway
how you got to live in manhattan plaza?
KIMAKO BARAKA   SONDRA ELAINE JONES

reached back 20 years in famous
artist brother's life. only the last
20 minutes of yours titillated
their imaginations.
he won an obie.
you sold amway.
they sell pulp.
and can't even say your name
cept to say his first.
SONDRA ELAINE   KIMAKO BARAKA   JONES

the only black lesbian in iowa city
calls manhattan late that night
wanting to know was it true
roi's sister was killed.
knew your name but couldn't say it.
felt the loss right on.
wanted connection.
became more afraid being given details.
was keeping the lights on all night.
checking the back seat of her car in
the morning.
i start at noises i hear every night
and don't want to be sleeping by myself
and call other women i know who live alone.

a day later:
29 year old klansman sentenced to death
for beating strangling hanging
19 year old black man two years before
'to show klan strength in alabama.'
not quite so amazing
as the 21 year old sadistic waif
you befriended
tried to save
two weeks before he grabbed you
round the neck by your shirt
drove a household knife
in your chest
deep in your head
and how'd you get to live in a
'luxury highrise' anyway?
KIMAKO   SONDRA ELAINE   BARAKA   JONES

was he an abused child? surely there was alcoholism in his fami-
ly? abandoned perhaps by his mother at an early age? or was he
crazy? or mean? did he just hate women? or did he just want
your jewelry and got mad cuz you resisted?

grimly famous artist brother asks:
'is this the way it happened?'
remembering perhaps mocking you in
Home.
you danced
acted
wrote
directed
dreamed right on

proselytizer
entrepreneur
cultural worker
fighter —
put up a 'ferocious struggle'
leaving 'swank manhattan pad'
a shambles.
and how'd you get to live there anyway
being only 'strayed,' 'little' sister
of famous artist brother
only SONDRA ELAINE JONES
only a black woman
KIMAKO.

sister of famous artist brother
stabbed to death
imagine the pain.

sister of famous artist brother
rolled out on a stretcher
oh what a shame.

sister of famous artist brother
in black body bag
oh what a drag.

(While the early reports of Kimako Baraka's murder were sensationalist, Thulani Davis, writer and editor, published a serious article on Kimako's life and work in the February 21, 1984 issue of *The Village Voice*.)

vii.

An exile I have loved tells me she's going home.
Smug I say:
    'Back to the city?'
    'No. First to Zambia. Then Zimbabwe.
    Finally Transvaal. Home,' she answers sad.
We sleep and wake to voices of men in the hallway
asking through doors of faces that are changed
and names that have not been spoken since.
I hold her to me
and remember the gold in my ears
ask for a way to stay in touch with her
tell her she's got a home long as I got mine.*
Hold her to me until she must push away
and slip from the room.

---

*Lines adapted from "I Left My Baby," *Jimmy Rushing: Sent For You Yesterday*
(Bluesway, reissued 1973).

living as a lesbian rambling

Cleo wants to break up with Doris. She confides to me:
'Truth be told sharing a bed with one body gets into
places the fucking don't. It makes for need where
there wasn't none. The sleeping together does. If I
leave Doris, I'll have to find somebody else to sleep
with. That's the drag of it all. The leaving that is.'

Doris writes Cleo a postcard from across the street:
'When I can't suck your pussy, I put sugar, cigarettes,
marijuana, caffeine, and alfalfa sprouts in my
mouth.'

And here I am here having been left. My body wants hers so
bad I am almost relieved she said no. And then goodbye. The
last Wallenda on the high wire that day the wind changed.

Withholding and demanding,
I never said *love* unless you said it first
and you never said *make love* unless
I said it first.
Still I traveled with trucks, tractor trailers, flat beds, campers,
cabs, wide and oversize loads to sleep with you. Whales log-
ging against medians. Swimmers of the great macadams. I sailed
their back winds, swerved to avoid their fish tails, jackknifes,
and blown-off treads, crashed their caravans, inhaled their
fumes to go to bed with you.

Our reunion was intended for this century. I know her from before. In the dream it is a desert or some other dusty, desolate place like southeast D.C. People walk and carry their houses on their backs. From North Carolina to Oklahoma, I want to know the Trail of Tears only to return to search the Great Smokies for those of my people who refused to leave.

I've gotten you confused with that runaway sister I shared a bed with who left me and my faithful half-brother to our incorrigible mother — grief so unrelenting she could not console us. My brother ran away to the army soon after. Too late for Korea he deserted and disappeared, his passion to draw numbed by whisky, fighting, and hatred of white men.

I'm travelin light.* My clothes could fit a matchbox.** I use a camera for passion. Away from the cities that knew us in this life. I cultivate the barrel cactus, prickly heart on green sleeve. Make pets of armadillos. Carry no medicine for snake bites. And hallucinate til you find me and make your pallet beside mine in these land-locked places our great grandmothers knew. In the 117 degree sun I am lonely and regret the times I was too defiant to come.

*"I'm Travelin' Light," as sung by Billie Holiday.
**"Billie's Blues," written and sung by Billie Holiday.

Outside a laundromat in chemical Elizabeth I follow a man rouged like my mother billowing yellow dress over dark camisole over rhythms measured and random hips like my mother forgetting I call *Mama* to him boldly sweetly he accepts my sadness takes my arm makes me sit with him pulls his hem to his crotch spreads his ample thighs and to my chapped lips kisses his palm full with the scent of yerba buena.

Pumpkins punctuate green hills. Off on a cliff above the ocean a lone palm tree sweeps the wind leaves akimbo and then redwoods tall as mountains. And she sends me a dozen yellow roses in Berkeley. The card says: 'And we can still be friends.'

Each day I wear one in my buttonhole or behind my ear. I wear the last one pinned to my green lapel. She nearly withers during the delay in Baltimore. I revive her in Newark. She spreads herself finally in a short glass of water with a wide mouth. I send her two pairs of my dirty bikini briefs and a scribbled poem in plain brown wrapper:
    'And that's how it is.
    Truth be told.
    I can't be without somebody to sleep with.
    It's the body.
    A woman's — must be a woman's.
    And yours was superb and particular
    for arms, legs, breasts
    supplanting the seduction of dreams.'

Pueblo Bonito

a dream of anger over too soon in a room
salvaged by some white man searching for a wall
of turquoise migrations and migrations
later
legends of early death from gum infection
an angry Navajo locked in a chamber of skulls
ancient as Africans
masonry a wonder
a ruin of old commerce
head between thighs
sweating and cold at sight of the grinding stone
short of breath from the anger
lingering after the dream over too soon
in a room of stone and ghosts of anger
throat dry from primordial stronghold
of mesas and buttes
longing for a place of wetness

triumph

I notice the disappearance of large things first.
Then left, at the last minute cast off things
too cumbersome to fit your matchbox.*
Empty closets.
Dust bold in relief of objects swept from
the dresser top.
Less visible artifacts to be discovered gone
later.

The African's first shock at her severance
from a familiar piece of earth
and an ocean of grief to cross
are what I am feeling this day.

I anticipate tonight not feeling your weight.

Too numb for anger yet.
Too afraid.
There's something familiar about this event.
It seems old.

Despite the foreshadowing
I am at this moment unbelieving.

Pretending to hear your car.
Predicting the phone will ring with a message
that what I am seeing is not what I am getting.

*From "Billie's Blues," as written and sung by Billie Holiday.

I'll yell rape.
It's that kind of emergency.
But there is no siren sounding.
Language is inaccessible.
No vision.
Only memory.

I stand back and watch me scream into a dial tone.

My sense of you is ever more powerful
than you ever were.
From this shore
I don't see how I will ever
get cross that ocean.

jazz poem for Morristown, N.J.

i pass so many dead things in the road
and grind my teeth in ecstasy
of contact
neck   middle   head
wild timid now dead
exquisite fuchsia expectorate
of entrail and brain
things
in the road.

curious . . . so many seeming sleeping
struck squash
dead decomposing
hash pink mush gray
gut exposing
things   SMASH!
in the road.

strutting crows like penguins
picking a flattened rabbit
on a curve in Piscataway, New Jersey
risking dying scattering at the whine
of my startled tread
returning to pick the carcass more.
diligent buzzards striating and peeling
back neat the skin of a doe
brought down by a pickup truck
and dragged to the shoulder of an Arizona road.

in Brooklyn
children laugh at sling shot
pigeon
inside out under car wheel dead.

sad . . . so many dead things in the road.
no powers of discernment
no antennas to cross the road
to the other side
in predatory industrial encroachment
not even Lenapes* in the wood
could have saved
so many things struck dead in the road.

intestine smeared medians of whole raccoon families.

vitriolic skunk dismembered.

decapitated cowardly possum.

*Native Americans who inhabited parts of what are now known as New
Jersey.

to Vanessa Williams: Miss America (black) 1984

When you play with the big boys
they will definitely fuck you.

living as a lesbian at 35

in my car I am fishing in my pocketbook
eyes on the road
for my wallet.
in my mind I am fishing in your drawers
eyes on the road
for your pussy.
high speeds evoke fucking.
depending on your mood you come.
it goes on:
I do too from you
over the wheel
hand between my thighs
eyes on the road
and the end of all: sex.

my mind:
a favored child has more freedom from her parents
a hippocampus more freedom from the horse and dolphin
a hippopotamus more freedom from her short legs
and muzzle
than my hypothalmus from lusting
and the end of all: sex.

my age?
the years I missed?
the women I had no opportunity with?
an old lover is sweet and good.
an old friend surprising and familiar.
all bodies possibilities.
any bodies.
lust, the cause of every tribute and transaction
for the end of all: sex.

to work to the end of day
to talk to the end of talk
to run to the end of dark
to have at the end of it all: sex.

the wish for forever
for more often
for more.

the promises
the absurdity
the histrionics
the loss of pride
the bargaining
the sadness after.

in wakefulness wanting
in wakefulness waiting.

marimba

awake on the edge of sleep
after brief absence
you are next to me inking my dreams
asleep on the edge of waking
i stumble among blind hunters left to
feel for their prey
pressed
strength fading
i plunge past their groping blows to yours
and drowsily refuse to lift my legs open
over the edge of the bed
until i am told
of the darkness of her stairwell
of how she smelled you
and came for you there
black camisole
fingers flexed
how you opened your skirt
pushed her on her back
stooped and spread your legs
for her mouth
lips dripping for it.

i hear a marimba player chanting
her slave song in portuguese.

lick me and cover me.
i am, i am in love with you.

Kittatinny

I wanna love and treat you, love and treat you right.

Bob Marley

Kittatinny Tunnel in that holy place you let me hit
I push on toward your darker part.
I'll take you there and mean it.

In my car, by the road, in a tent, in a pit
stop, and practice a funkier art,
Kittatinny Tunnel of that holy place you let me hit.

Shout, cry, promise, beg, cajole, go limp, or spit
on me with dirty words to test my heart.
I'll take you there and mean it.

Crawl from me, pitch a fit,
stand, hug the wall, bend, and direct me part
and penetrate Kittatinny, that holy place you let me hit.

And take it, take it, take it.
Call it bitch, whore, slave, tart.
I'll take you there and mean it.

Tribad, dildo, lick your clit-
oris. Come, pee, shit, or fart,
I'll take you there and mean it,
Kittatinny Tunnel of that holy place you let me hit.

Other titles from Firebrand Books include:

The Big Mama Stories by Shay Youngblood/$8.95

A Burst Of Light, Essays by Audre Lorde/$7.95

Diamonds Are A Dyke's Best Friend by Yvonne Zipter/$9.95

Dykes To Watch Out For, Cartoons by Alison Bechdel/$6.95

Eye Of A Hurricane, Stories by Ruthann Robson / $8.95

The Fires Of Bride, A Novel by Ellen Galford/$8.95

A Gathering Of Spirit, A Collection by North American Indian Women edited by Beth Brant *(Degonwadonti)*/$9.95

Getting Home Alive by Aurora Levins Morales and Rosario Morales/$8.95

Good Enough To Eat, A Novel by Lesléa Newman/$8.95

Humid Pitch, Narrative Poetry by Cheryl Clarke/$8.95

Jonestown & Other Madness, Poetry by Pat Parker/$5.95

The Land Of Look Behind, Prose and Poetry by Michelle Cliff/$6.95

A Letter To Harvey Milk, Short Stories by Lesléa Newman/$8.95

Letting In The Night, A Novel by Joan Lindau/$8.95

Making It, A Woman's Guide to Sex in the Age of AIDS by Cindy Patton and Janis Kelly/$3.95

Metamorphosis, Reflections On Recovery, by Judith McDaniel/$7.95

Mohawk Trail by Beth Brant *(Degonwadonti)*/$6.95

Moll Cutpurse, A Novel by Ellen Galford/$7.95

More Dykes To Watch Out For, Cartoons by Alison Bechdel/$7.95

The Monarchs Are Flying, A Novel by Marion Foster/$8.95

My Mama's Dead Squirrel, Lesbian Essays on Southern Culture by Mab Segrest/$8.95

The Other Sappho, A Novel by Ellen Frye/$8.95

Politics Of The Heart, A Lesbian Parenting Anthology edited by Sandra Pollack and Jeanne Vaughn/$11.95

Presenting. . .Sister NoBlues by Hattie Gossett/$8.95

A Restricted Country by Joan Nestle/$8.95

Sanctuary, A Journey by Judith McDaniel/$7.95

Sans Souci, And Other Stories by Dionne Brand/$8.95

Shoulders, A Novel by Georgia Cotrell/$8.95

The Sun Is Not Merciful, Short Stories by Anna Lee Walters/$7.95

Tender Warriors, A Novel by Rachel Guido deVries/$7.95

This Is About Incest by Margaret Randall/$7.95

The Threshing Floor, Short Stories by Barbara Burford/$7.95

Trash, Stories by Dorothy Allison/$8.95

The Women Who Hate Me, Poetry by Dorothy Allison/$5.95

Words To The Wise, A Writer's Guide to Feminist and Lesbian Periodicals & Publishers by Andrea Fleck Clardy/$3.95

Yours In Struggle, Three Feminist Perspectives on Anti-Semitism and Racism by Elly Bulkin, Minnie Bruce Pratt, and Barbara Smith/$8.95

You can buy Firebrand titles at your bookstore, or order them directly from the publisher (141 The Commons, Ithaca, New York 14850, 607-272-0000).

Please include $1.75 shipping for the first book and $.50 for each additional book.

A free catalog is available on request.